# Constructing a Fireplace Mantel

## Step-by-Step from Plywood and Stock Moldings

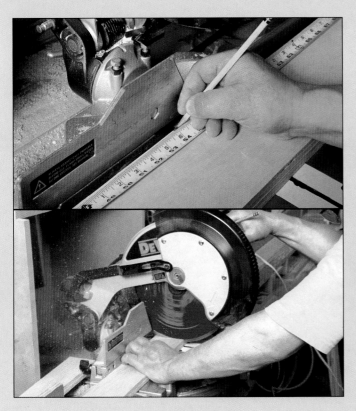

Steve Penberthy with
Lawrence S. Welsh

Schiffer Publishing Ltd

4880 Lower Valley Road, Atglen, PA 19310 USA

# Contents

Acknowledgments ................................................................ 3

Introduction ...................................................................... 4

The Mantel ........................................................................ 5

Building the Mantel ............................................................. 9

Finishing .......................................................................... 56

Decorative Accents ............................................................. 63

Gallery ............................................................................. 68

Gallery of Finished Mantels ................................................. 73

Sources of Supply .............................................................. 80

Published by Schiffer Publishing Ltd.
4880 Lower Valley Road
Atglen, PA 19310
Phone: (610) 593-1777; Fax: (610) 593-2002
E-mail: Info@schifferbooks.com

For the largest selection of fine reference books on this and related subjects, please visit our web site at
**www.schifferbooks.com**
We are always looking for people to write books on new and related subjects. If you have an idea for a book please contact us at the above address.

This book may be purchased from the publisher.
Include $3.95 for shipping.
Please try your bookstore first.
You may write for a free catalog.

In Europe, Schiffer books are distributed by
Bushwood Books
6 Marksbury Ave.
Kew Gardens
Surrey TW9 4JF England
Phone: 44 (0) 20 8392-8585; Fax: 44 (0) 20 8392-9876
E-mail: info@bushwoodbooks.co.uk
Website: www.bushwoodbooks.co.uk
Free postage in the U.K., Europe; air mail at cost.

# Acknowledgments

Woodworking has been my life's work. Born into a family of lumbermen and women, I suppose that I was molded to it from an early age. I thoroughly love the work, but it's the people that are the true joy.

My heartfelt thanks go out to my fellow workers at Pine Mountain Lumber in Yreka, California and Penberthy Lumber in Los Angeles, your help and guidance have served me well. The good people at Woodcrafters in Portland, Oregon, are a source of pride and inspiration to me. Thomas Penberthy drew the first mantel layout pages; Robert Markley's illustrations bring the mantel to life. Jeff Metke of Metke Woodworking in Lake Oswego, Oregon, provided photographs of his company's work. Thanks also to Spray Kote of Milwaukee, Oregon. Larry Welsh, without your knowledge and skill this project could not have been done.

My parents, Mary and Fay Penberthy, set a high standard for fairness and hard work. My children, Laurie and Matt bless me with their exuberance for life. Charles R. Meyer has unselfishly lent his helpful ear for many years. My true love, my bride of thirty-three years, Peggy Penberthy, sets me off each day with a spring in my step and joy in my heart. Thanks.

— Steve Penberthy


Like any complex project or endeavor, a book requires the input and efforts of many. With that said I wish to acknowledge Steve Penberthy for his encouragement, forethought, and direction, Carl Paasche and Robert Freeman for their insights into design and technique, and for lending a critical eye to my work, and my shop partner, Bob Jeffries, for his help in managing Woodcrafters millwork shop. Thanks, as well, to the rest of my Woodcrafters associates, whose unselfish help was instrumental in completing this book.

Finally, but not least, I wish to thank my parents, Mary Lou and John Welsh, for the guidance, love, and wisdom they have instilled in me.

— Larry Welsh

# Introduction

If you've been thinking that your fireplace could use some dressing up, but you've given up on the idea because you think that building a mantel is too hard or too expensive, this book is for you. The assembly methods shown in this book will make it easy for you to build the mantel of your dreams....at a price that you can afford.

The fireplace and mantel are always the focal point of a room. It usually reflects the architecture of the home as well as the individual style of the occupant. The mantel's design and finish, whether stone, brick, hardwood or softwood, painted or stained, set the mood and establish the flavor of a room.

This book will help you build the fireplace mantel that best fits your home. My company builds many mantels each year. We build them to suit our customer's wishes. Although I've chosen a popular design, the construction methods are the same for an endless variety of styles.

On seeing one of our mantels, probably the first question you would have would concern the cost. Built to order cabinetry isn't cheap. However, this mantel is made affordable by building it from readily available hardwood plywood and moldings. Plywood offers stability when exposed to the nearby heat source while offering a wide selection of face veneers that will match your decor. Moldings are the decorative accents that personalize your mantel. We are building this mantel in maple. The plywood and stock molding in these profiles should be available near you.

Stock moldings are used to "dress up" the mantel. There are hundreds of patterns available in many species. Because the expensive, time consuming, millwork has been done, the only tools you will need are saws to cut-to-length, size and miter.

Hopefully you will be able to find the plywood and molding at your local hardwood specialty store, local lumber yard or even at one of the large home improvement stores. If your access is limited please refer to the source of supply page at the end of the book. If all fails please give me a call at Woodcrafters, Portland, OR. 800-777-3709 or e-mail woodcrafters.us@comcast.net. Thank you for purchasing the book.

We're here to help!

Steve Penberthy
212 N.E. Sixth Avenue
Portland, OR 97232

# The Mantel

## Suggested
## Tools & Supplies

Tablesaw
Tablesaw sled
Measuring tape
Miter saw
Nailer
Sander and paper
Clamps - adjustable 3700 series 8-10
Blue tape
Bar clamps - 8'
8" try square
Access to a planer
Hold down devices
Spray gun or access to a spray booth
Wood stain and top coat finish for hand finish
Spring clamps
Router bits - Amana

### S4S Lumber
Leg Stiles - (4) 3/4" x 1-1/2" x 54"
Leg Rails - (4) 3/4" x 2-1/2" x 4"
Leg Rails - 3/4" x 4-1/2" x 4"
Breast Plate Stiles - (2) 3/4" x 2-1/2" x 60"
Breast Plate Rails - (4) 3/4" x 2" x 60"
Feet - (2) 3/4" x 6" x 6-1/2"

### Moldings
M-610 Crown - 9'
M-1500 Lentil - 9'
M-1600 Half Round - 9'
M-1610 Quarter Round - 50'

### 3/4" Plywood (2 sheets, 4' x 8')
Breast Plate - (1) 13-3/4" x 60"
Leg Fronts - (2) 5" x 54"
Outside Leg - (2) 3-1/4" x 54"
Inside Leg - (2) 3-1/4" x 40"
Inside Breast Plate - (1) 3-1/4" x 61-1/2"
Top - (2) 7" x 79-1/2"
Inside Breast Plate Face - (2) 1-1/2" x 14"

S4S Maple
3/4" x 1-1/2"
3/4" x 2-1/2"
3/4" x 7-1/4"

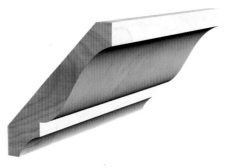

M-610 Maple Crown
5/8" x 3-1/2"

M-1600 Maple 1/2 Round
3/8" x 1/2"

M-1610 Maple 1/4 Round
1/2" x 1/2"

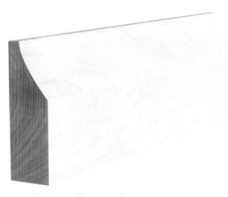

M-1500 Maple Lentil
1/2" x 1-1/2"

# Measurements of the Fireplace

The first step in planning your fireplace mantel is to determine the set back from your heat source. Local building codes are the primary rule to follow. Owner's manuals, for gas fireplaces and inserts, wood-burning, pellet, and kerosene stoves, will provide guidelines for set-back dimensions. Please check that your local codes are met. These set backs are for your protection. Please take the time to understand them. They are an integral part of the build of your mantel.

The following illustrations give you the "foundation" dimensions for laying out the size of your mantel. Figure 1. represents your wall, firebox and hearth. The dotted line represents the code required set back from the firebox. Your mantel may be further away from this line, but no closer.

Figure 2.represents a typical hearth, firebox and tile or brick surround that you might find in your home. Measure and record the dimensions, marked as "AA" thru "GG", found on your job. Use these dimensions to "fit" your mantle to the surroundings. The boxed measurements represent the firebox, H is height, W is width. As in figure 1, you will establish the code-mandated minimum set back from the firebox, top and sides, using the dimensions in the boxes as starting points. With these dimensions in mind you are ready to plan your mantels size.

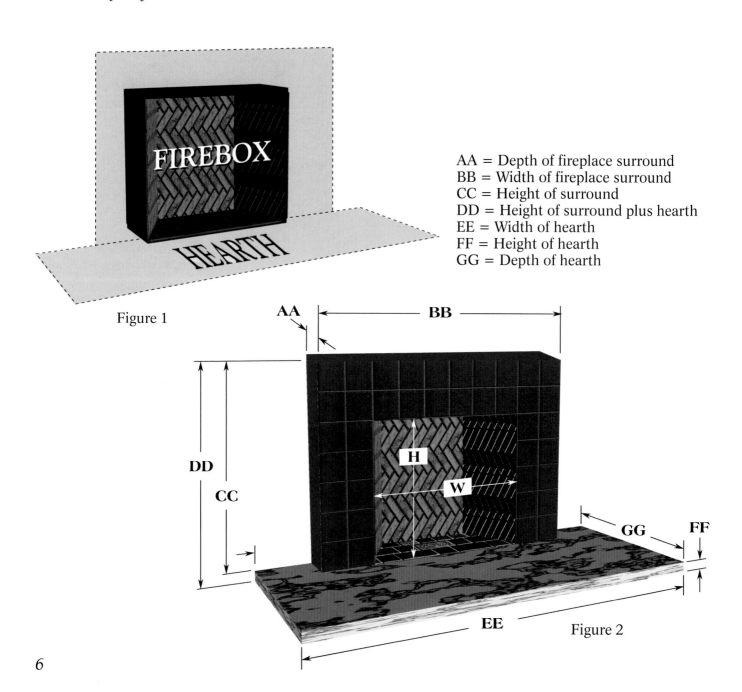

AA = Depth of fireplace surround
BB = Width of fireplace surround
CC = Height of surround
DD = Height of surround plus hearth
EE = Width of hearth
FF = Height of hearth
GG = Depth of hearth

Figure 1

Figure 2

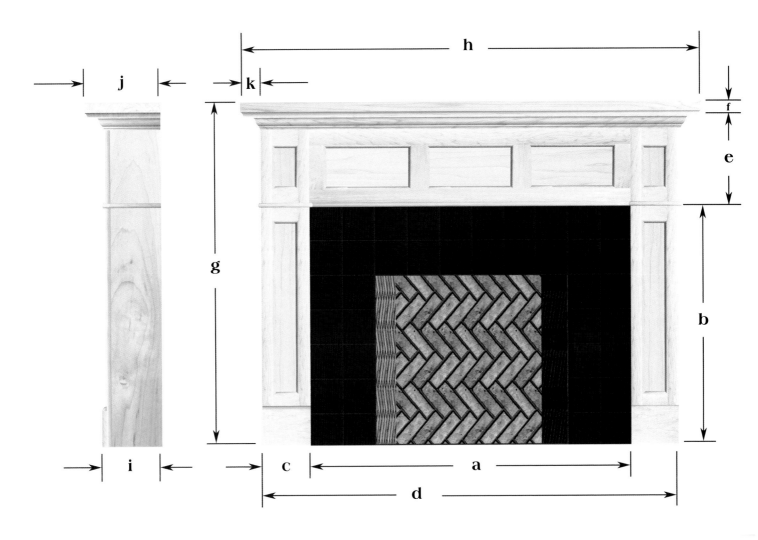

a = inside width of the mantel
b = inside height of the mantel
c = the mantel leg width
d = a + c + c
e = breastplate height
f = thickness of mantel shelf
g = b + e + f
h = length of mantel shelf, d + k + k
i = depth of leg
j = depth of mantel shelf
k = side overhang of mantel shelf, without molding

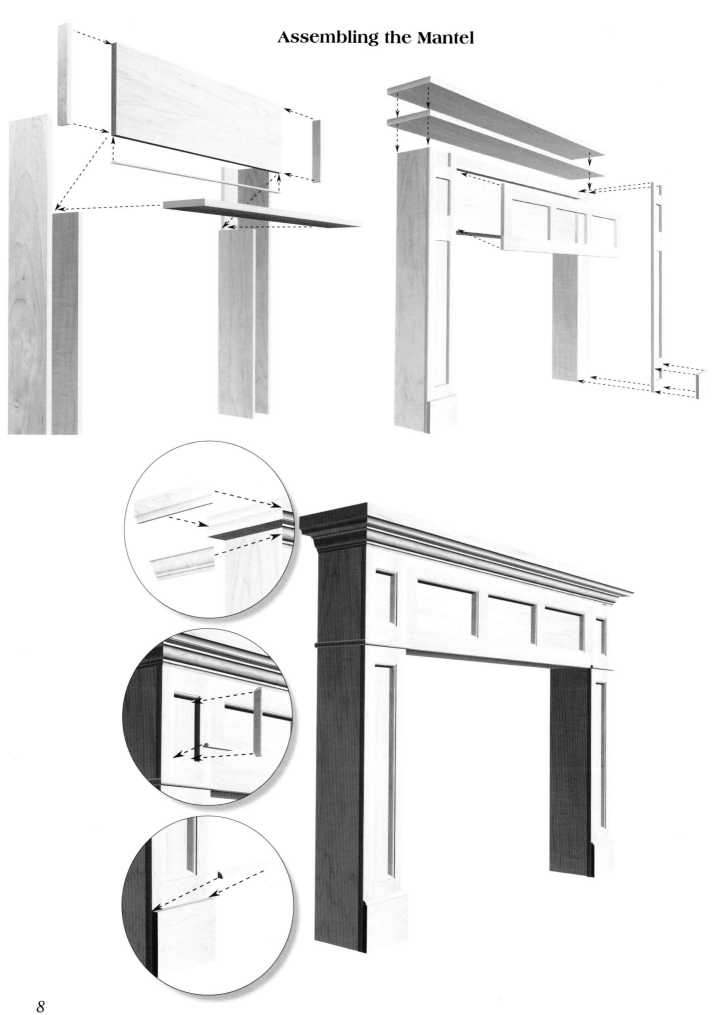

# Assembling the Mantel

# Building the Mantel

Choose a piece of plywood with no voids, defects in the veneer, shipping damage, or scratches.

Set the saw fence for the cut. For cutting plywood be sure your saw is properly equipped with a splitter and guard and use a good combination blade or a plywood blade.

If you are considering staining the mantel, grain is also important. Since the main focus of attention is the **breastplate,** or the large horizontal centerpiece of the mantel, I choose that first, looking for a nice swatch of grain. On this piece of plywood it is in this area, so I will lay out my cuts with that in mind.

Make the first cut, defining one edge of the breastplate.

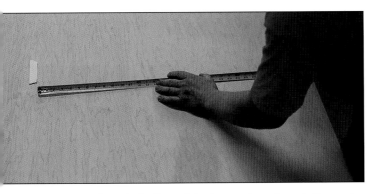

Measure and mark the line of the breastplate. I mark the spot with a piece of tape.

Set your fence to 13 3/4" and cut the other edge of the breastplate. The finished breastplate, with a 1/4" trim piece on the bottom edge, will be 14" tall.

Put the remaining pieces together and choose the best grain for the **front of the legs**.

For the initial cut on the leg, the fence is set at 6". With a final cut bringing the width to 5", this allows us to get clean, "virgin" edges on both sides. Make the cut with the mill edge against the fence.

Repeat with the second piece.

Make the second cut at 5", keeping the previously cut edge against the fence and removing the mill edge. Do the same with the other piece.

Next set the fence to 3 1/4" and cut the sides of the legs. It should be noted here that the inside of the legs may require adjustment to fit the fireplace surround. For this mantel we are assuming that the mantel fits flush against the wall, and that the outer and inner sides of the legs will be the same depth.

A smaller piece is needed for the **sides at the top of the inner legs**. Grain is not critical here, so we rip a piece of plywood at 1 1/2".

Finally, cut a piece at 1 3/4" for the **bottom of the breastplate**.

Make the first cut using a cross-cut sled. We prefer the sled to a radial arm saw. The use of the table saw results in a more precise cut. You will appreciate the "tight" fit when assembling the mantel.

The **mantel shelf,** or top, requires another half sheet of plywood. Rip two pieces at 7", to allow for a double thickness top.

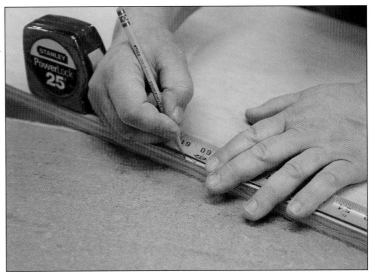

Measure 60" and mark.

The **breastplate** will be 60" wide. Returning to the grain pattern chosen earlier, center your rule on it and mark 30" to either side. At this point it is approximate, though you will cut to exactly 60" on the table saw.

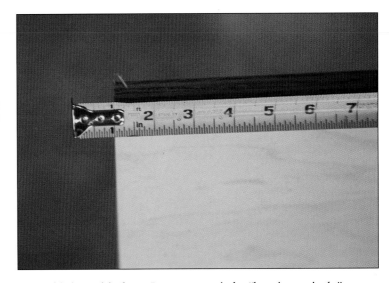

Since this is a critical cut, I measure again by "burning an inch." This simply means that instead of using the tape measure's hook, I align the 1" mark with the end of the board ...

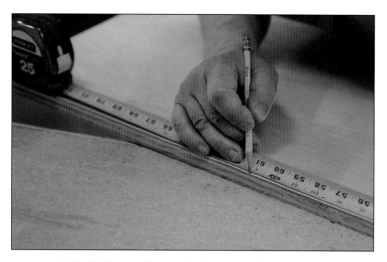

and check that my first mark lines up with 61". This will correct for a hook that is bent out of shape.

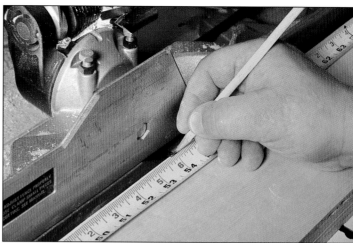

From that cut measure 54". This too is a critical cut so double check the measurement using the "burn an inch" technique.

When all is correct, place the wood in the sled and carefully make the cut.

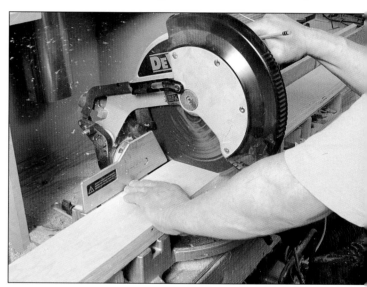

By lining up the ends, I can cut two pieces at the same time, insuring that they are the same length.

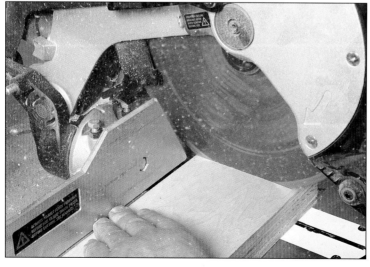

At the chop saw, make a clean cut near one end of the **leg fronts**. I like to make my own clean starting point. Some hardwood looks square or "clean," but is slightly off. Trust your cut, not someone else's.

Cut the mill end off the **outer sides** of the legs.

Use the leg fronts to mark the length of the outer sides of the legs.

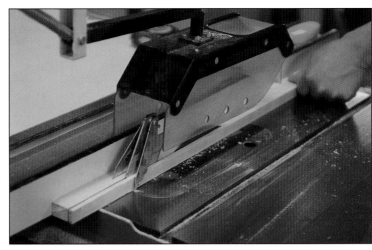

When things are right, rip the edge trim.

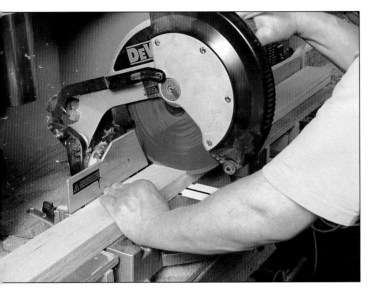

Line up on end and cut the other.

Make a fresh cut on one end of the breastplate edge trim.

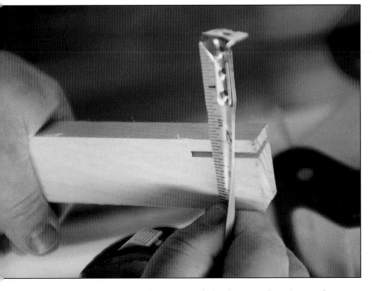

**The finished bottom edge trim of the breastplate** is cut from 1x2. First rip a 1/4" x 3/4" strip from it. Cut in just a bit to check the dimensions.

Holding the cut end against the bottom edge of the breastplate mark the other.

Chop it off.

When the glue is dried on the breastplate trim piece, use 120 sandpaper to even the edges. Hold the sander flat so as not to round over the edge.

Apply a bead of glue to the bottom edge of the breastplate.

Sand the whole breastplate face with 120 grit paper.

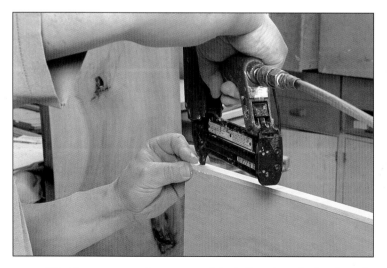

Working your way from one end, tack the edge trim in place. In this case I put the table saw cut edge against the breastplate, leaving the mill edge exposed. Clean up any excess glue. **Note:** if you don't have a power nailer, this can be done with a hammer and small finish nails. It is suggested however that you pre-drill the trim piece to avoid splitting.

Repeat with 150 grit. Sanding the breastplate is easier at this stage, and allows me to find any defects I may have missed initially and correct them before I invest more time and money.

Mark the 1 1/2" wide piece cut for the **top of the inner leg** to the height of the breastplate.

Cut the biscuit mortices in the ends of the breastplate...

Chop it off, and repeat for the other leg.

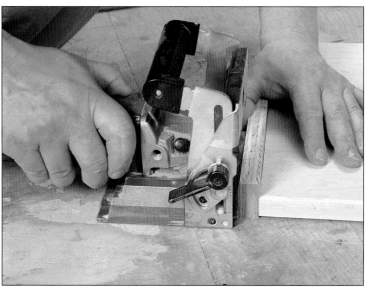

and the side of the leg pieces. I am holding the leg piece against the breastplate for support during the process.

Three #20 biscuits hold the top of the inner leg to the breastplate. Holding the piece in place, mark the centers for each of the biscuits on the breastplate and the leg pieces. I generally space one bisquit at 1/2" in from each edge and a third in the center.

Place the #20 biscuits in place...

and dry fit the joint.

Nail it in place.

Before gluing the leg piece to the breastplate, I have found it best to attach the top of the inner leg to the edge of the leg front. After confirming which is the face side of the leg front, apply glue at the top portion of the leg edge.

Apply clamps until the glue dries. If you do not have a nailer available, this step can be accomplished using only clamps.

Align the top of the inner leg so it is flush with the top and the face of the leg front.

When the glue has dried, remove the clamps. I add a piece of painter's tape to the front edge of the breastplate. If there is any glue seepage, the tape will protect the wood. Any glue left on the mantel will be invisible or nearly so until the finishing stage, when it will block the absorption of stain or finish and leave an unsightly blemish.

Dry fit the legs to the breastplate.

Apply glue to the biscuit mortice in the leg.

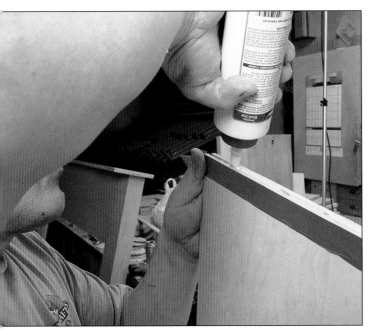

When gluing, I work with the breastplate first, while my hands are relatively clean. This is a time to be very careful of the glue or you will end up spending much more time cleaning up. Apply glue to the biscuit mortice in the breastplate.

As before, spread it with sandpaper.

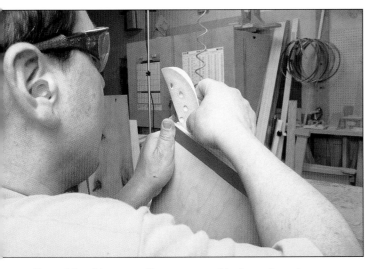

Spread it with an applicator or an old piece of sandpaper.

Apply glue to the biscuits themselves. From this point you must move quickly. The glue makes the biscuit swell so it must be seated without delay.

Insert the biscuits in the leg.

Check square by measuring at the base of the legs…

Align the leg with the breastplate and seat the biscuits.

and just under the breastplate. They should be within 1/8" of each other. Anything more will be noticeable.

Clamp the legs to the breastplate.

As an alternative to clamping, you can use a nailer to fasten the legs to the breastplate, coming in from the side. Be sure to keep the nailer level so that the nail does not break through the front of the breastplate.

Progress front…

Spread the glue out evenly.

and back.

Slide the carcass back on the table so there is a lip of the table showing. Align the **leg side** with the **leg front**, using a square to properly situate it. Nail it in place.

With the edge of the leg hanging over the table, apply a glue line along the outside edge. I use my forefinger as a guide so the glue is applied to the center of the edge.

I try to use as few nails as are necessary to get a good joint. At the top, however, I can put two nails, because this will be covered by molding.

About half way down the height of the breastplate I put another nail for strength.

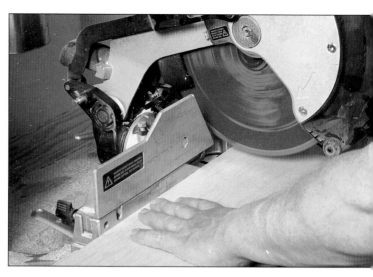

Moving to the **mantel shelf**, with the best side up, make a clean cut at one end.

Another nail can go at a point level with the bottom of the breastplate, since this, too, will have a molding.

Measure from the fresh cut and cut the top to length. In this case it is 79-1/2".

From there down I place a nail every 8 to 10 inches, checking for a good tight joint.

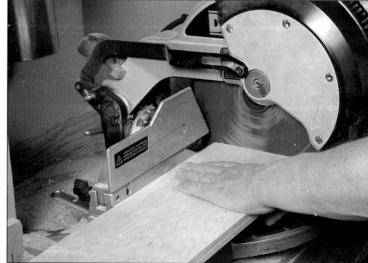

Chop it off cleanly

Before attaching the mantel shelf, notice that the breastplate sags from its own weight. It needs to be square when the shelf is attached.

To get it square, these props or shims can be added. Make adjustments to get the shelf as flat as possible.

With the mantel shelf turned over *so the top surface is against the carcass*, center it on the carcass and mark the its outline on the shelf.

Turn the shelf so the marks you made are on the top and properly aligned. This should give you a good nailing line in the next step. The nails will be covered by the second top piece.

A scrap piece can be marked to help keep things square as you glue and nail. First rest it on the front of the leg and mark to the edge of the mantel shelf.

Both marks.

The first line.

Apply a bead of glue to the top of the carcass. Even though there will be a molding here, it is always a good idea to follow "good glue hygiene" and apply it with care, cleaning up any overflow.

Next move it to just inside the leg and mark again at the edge of the shelf.

Align the mantel shelf to the carcass using the lines drawn earlier and double checking with a ruler. Starting at one corner and using the gauge to assure the proper line, nail the shelf in place

Work your way across the mantle top, nailing every six or eight inches. You will find the gauge most useful.

As before, make a fresh cut at one end of the second mantel shelf piece.

When you have nailed across the top, check the sides for square and nail in place.

Align the fresh cut with one end of the attached shelf piece and mark the length at the other.

Now add nails to insure good glue adhesion.

With the good side of the shelf facing up, cut to length.

Apply glue to the underside of the top mantel shelf.

An alternative to nailing is to clamp the top shelf piece in place.

Align it…

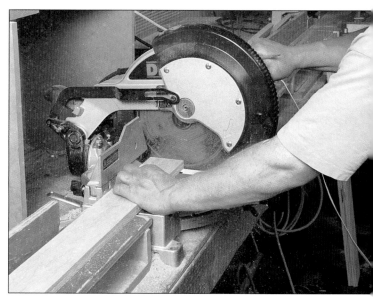

Now we move to the **inside legs**. Make a fresh cut at one end of an inside leg piece.

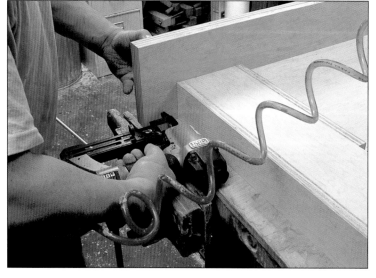

and nail it in place from underneath. The nail should be close enough to the carcass to be covered by the crown molding.

Hold the piece in place against the carcass and mark the other end.

Cut to length.

Align the inner leg side…

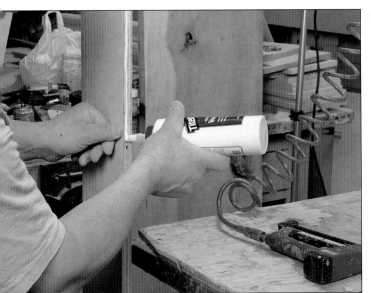

Apply a bead of glue to the inside edge of the leg...

and nail it in place.

and spread it evenly.

Repeat on the other leg.

The final carcass piece is the return on the underside of the breastplate. After cutting a fresh end, lay the piece on the tops of the inner leg sides and mark the length. Chop it off to length.

Put it in place.

Apply a bead of glue at the top of the legs…

Secure to the top of the legs.

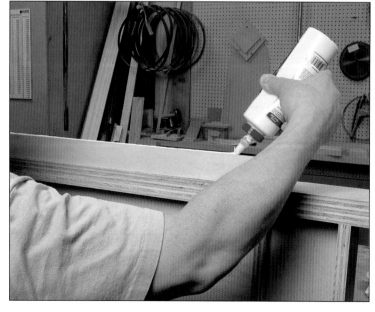

and another along the edge that joins with the back of the breastplate.

Turn the mantel upside down and secure from the front, aligning things as you go. These nails line will be covered by trim.

Scribe a line to mark the underside of the crown molding.

Cut the stile pieces from 3/4" x 1-1/2" maple. We will rip to width and plane. The **leg stiles** need to be 1-1/4" wide and 1/2" deep. I rip them on the table saw at 1-5/16" leaving 1/16" for planing.

Plane the width first. With maple it is best to do this with several shallow passes, going with the grain so as not to rip it out.

The **other trim pieces** are standard widths, 2-1/2" and 4-1/2", so we can move directly to planing. In this case I will only need to plane one side to bring it down from 3/4" to 1/2". I plane away the back side. Again, plane at small increments to reduce the chance of tear-out, which is also helped by feeding them into the planer at a slight angle.

In preparation for applying the trim moldings, sand the front surface of each leg. Not only is this the best time to get at areas that will later be recessed, it flushes the joints between the leg's sides and front. Start with 150 grit, followed by 220.

Mark the stile trim piece for the outside edge of the leg and cut to length. This piece goes from the bottom of the leg to the top. Repeat for all four stiles.

Mark the line of the bottom of the breastplate across the legs.

When applying the stiles, I begin with the inside ones to allow for easier access later on. To install the stile to the legs, apply a bead of glue on the back of the stile.

Spread the glue. Again, it is important to be careful of too much glue. Extra care here will save hours of time later on.

A block is used to keep the stile flush with the edge of the leg. Hold the block in place, pull the stile toward it, and nail. Try to place most of your nails in spots that will be covered up, such as under the crown, at the foot, and where the small trim piece runs across at the bottom of the breastplate. (see picture of completed trim)

Apply the inner stile to the other leg. This angle gives a little better view of the block in use. With only the inner stiles in place, we fit the rails.

Put a good square cut on one end of each of the rail trim pieces. Take your time here so you get no tear-out.

The upper rail is 2 1/2" wide. Its top edge will be 1/2" above the lower line of the crown molding to give a nailing surface; its bottom edge will be 2" below the crown. Measure up from the line of the crown 1/2" and mark.

Carry the line across the leg front.

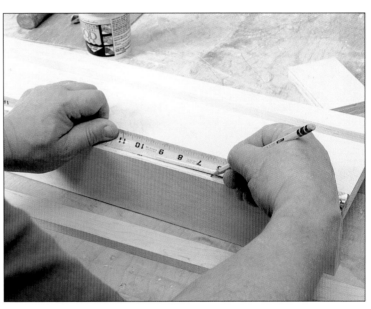

Carry the line across to the inner stile and repeat on the other leg.

The bottom rail is at the top of the foot. The foot will be 6" high, so mark the leg at that point.

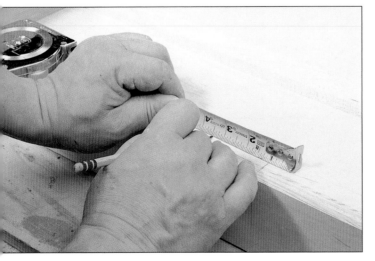

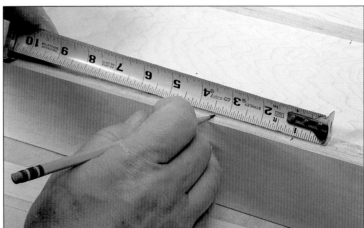

Move down to the line of the lower edge of the breastplate. The rail here is 4 1/2" wide. This time we will measure up 2 1/2" from the line, allowing for a 1/2" trim piece carried over from the breastplate and a 2" reveal above and below it.

Mark at 2 1/2" above the foot mark…

and draw a line. This will be the top edge of the bottom rail. This rail is 4 1/2" wide and will have a 2" reveal at the top, a 1/2" molding, and 2" hidden behind the foot, acting as a nailing surface.

Moving down to the breastplate line, carefully align the outer stile and hold the 4 1/2" rail stock in place. Mark it. It is good to give this a generous cut, because you can always come back and shave a little off.

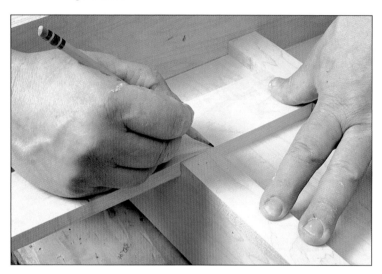

Hold the 2 1/2" upper rail stock in position against the installed inside stile, and use the loose outer stile to mark the finished width of the rail.

In fact this cut was a little too generous, so I need to go back and trim it down.

Cut and fit. It is best to do each of the rails individually and sequentially. This allows you to adjust for natural variances in the wood and gives a nice tight joint.

The second time is a charm.

Repeat the process at the foot.

Before gluing and nailing the rails, I like to double check both the placement and their squareness.

One at each end should do.

Apply glue to the back of the rail. It is wise to use as few nails as possible since the holes will be filled, not covered.

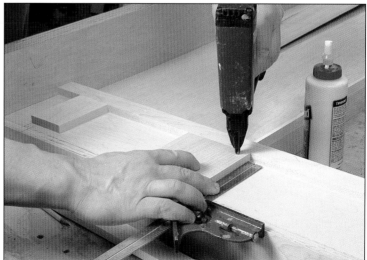

The use of a square during nailing helps insure the proper alignment. This wider piece requires more nails. One in the lower corner…

31

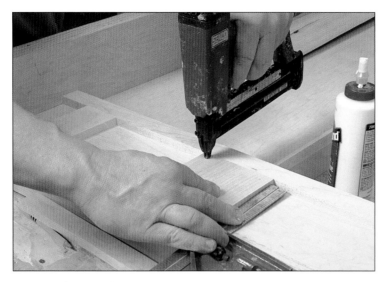

and one in the upper.

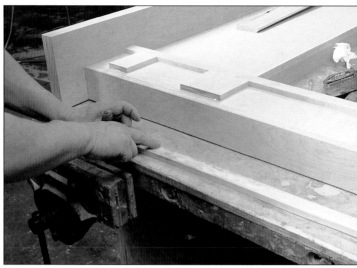

Apply glue to the back of the outer stile and spread it evenly.

The lower rail will also need four nails.

Holding the outer stile in place, nail from the top down. Again, the block will help with alignment.

Put a small bead of glue on the ends of the rails.

One leg stiled and railed. Repeat on the other leg.

Remark the depth of the crown on the front of the leg at the outside edge...

Use scrap plywood to mark the depth of the leg at the breast-plate. This will be used to set the table saw.

and the inside edge. Repeat on the other leg.

For the nailer set the saw at 1 7/8".

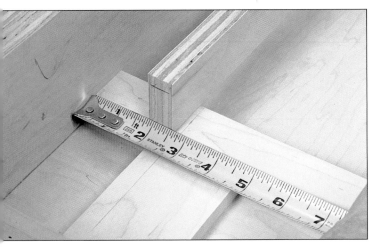

We secure the crown to the mantel with a filler piece. It will be 3/4" plywood and will leave a 1/16" to 1/8" reveal of crown. We attach the filler piece to the mantel by using a nailer strip. The width of this nailer can be determined by holding the filler inside the line of the crown and measuring. In this case it will be 1 7/8". The nailer will be ripped from 3/4" plywood.

Rip the 3/4" plywood.

Take the piece of scrap used to mark the depth of the leg for the filler and rip it to the mark.

Mark the **nailer strip** and cut it to length.

Test it on the mantel and make adjustments

After making a squaring cut on the filler piece, bring it back to the mantel and mark an accurate length.

When the fit is flush, rip the filler piece.

Chop it off.

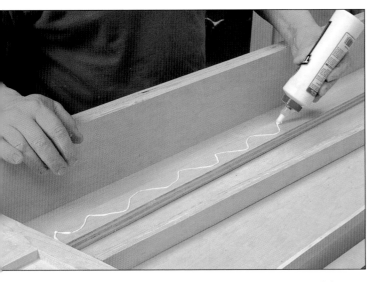

Apply a bead of glue to the back of the nailer and smooth it out.

Spread it evenly.

Align the nailer at the top of the breastplate and nail in place.

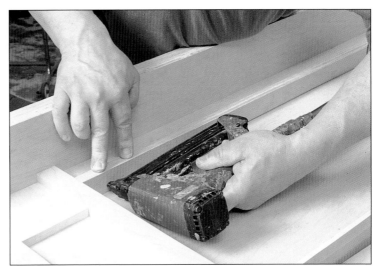

Hold the filler piece in place. Apply pressure to bring it snug against the breastplate and nail it. The nails should be kept low so they will be covered by the rail of the breastplate.

Apply glue to the bottom edge of the nailer and on the breastplate.

The lower line of the upper rail on the breastplate should continue the one on the leg. Carry that line around to the inner leg.

Measure from the filler piece to the line. In this case it is 2 1/8". This is the width of the upper rail in the breastplate.

Plane all the piece to the proper thickness and width.

The trim pieces for the breastplate will all be 1/2" thick. The rail at the top will have a finished size of 2-1/8", but I will rip it at 2-3/16" so I can plane the revealed edge. The lower rail is the milled width of 2-1/2", which allows for a 1/2" molding piece.

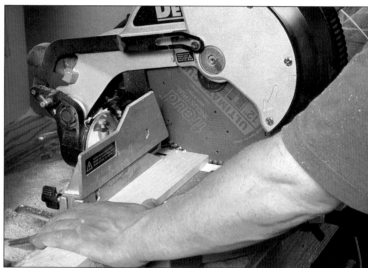

Square cut the upper rail.

The stiles are 2" and I am ripping them at 2-1/16" to allow for planning.

Hold it in place and mark it a little full. Chop it off and make small adjustments until the fit is snug.

Before applying the trim pieces, give the breastplate a final sanding with 220 grit paper.

Use the fewest nails necessary to hold the rail down.

Also sand the fitted rails and stiles before applying. There is much better access to them when they are loose than there will be later.

Square cut the lower rail, then mark its length. Again, keep it a little generous.

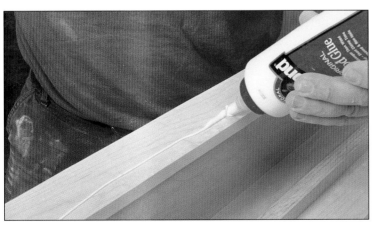

Apply glue to the backside of the top rail.

Trim until the fit is snug.

37

Before attaching the lower rail we will cut the four stiles for the breastplate trim. They are done in the same way as the leg rails. Square one end.

Test fit.

Start at one end of the breastplate. With the lower rail in place mark the length of the stile.

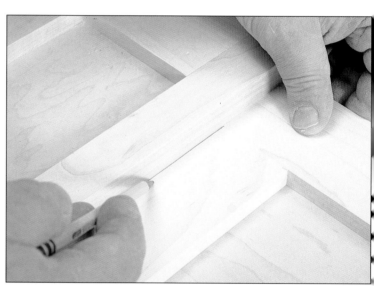

Sometimes you may find a gap, as we did here, where the stile meets the leg.

Chop to length.

A simple solution is to relief the back edge of the stile using sand paper.

The edge is now flush.

Though a bit more unusual, you may decide to have a smaller center panel with a tile insert or decorative piece, and larger outside panels. There are no rules. Pick something you like and go for it!

When the first stile is fitted it is a good time to establish the proportions of the panels in the breastplate. Rough cut the other stiles and simply move them around until you find a pattern that fits your needs. The first is three equal segments.

We'll go with the even design. Put the stiles in place...

Another possibility is to have smaller outside panels and a larger central panel.

and mark them for length.

Fit the stiles.

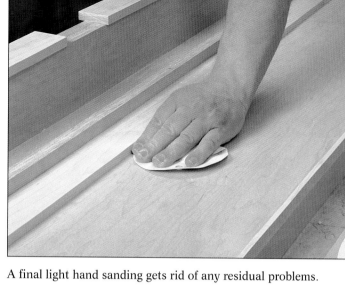

A final light hand sanding gets rid of any residual problems.

Ready for glue and nails.

Glue and nail the outer stiles first.

Sand using 220 grit paper.

Follow this up with the two inside stiles, checking again for position. Use a square during nailing.

Glue the lower rail.

The feet will be of 3/4" maple ripped to 6" wide.

Starting at one end pull the rail snug against the stiles and nail in place.

After squaring an end, mark the width of the foot...

Work your way to the other end.

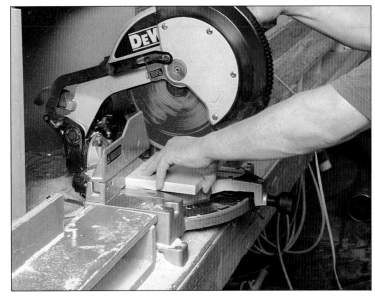

and chop it off. Do the same for the other leg.

Carefully fit the foot to the leg.

Dry fit the foot once again.

Before gluing and nailing fill the bottom space between the stiles with scrap 1/2" maple. It doesn't need to be pretty! You could use any 1/2" thick dry scrap stock. Glue and nail the filler in place.

Mark the correct position.

Sand the lower leg before applying the foot. A tight fit is a beautiful thing!

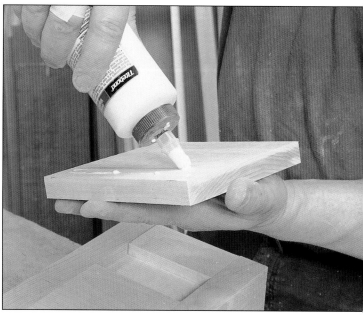

Apply and spread glue.

Align carefully...

and nail in place.

Before sanding the outside and face of the legs I want to fill the nailholes. Since this is tight-grained maple, I can do this pretty casually. If, however, it were oak or mahogany or any other open grained wood I would be much more careful. In those woods the filler tends to migrate into the grain and makes sanding and finishing much more difficult.

When putting filler into a joint like this, I mask off the surfaces to keep the filler out. Sanding in these corners is difficult, and this minimizes the necessity to do so. Once the filler is applied you can remove the tape. This is one of those little tricks that can save hours of sanding.

For now I'll just sand the areas adjoining the crown.

With the crown held in place mark the side of the leg at one end.

At the miter saw turn the molding upside down and backwards and make a 45 degree cut.

Mark the length of the return.

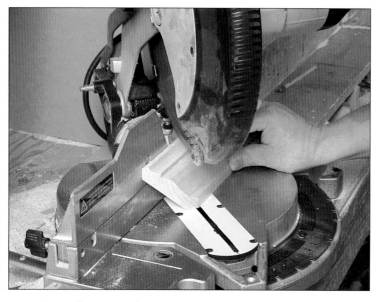

Reset the saw to the opposite 45 degree angle and cut the end piece off to fit the main piece as a return.

Reset the miter to 90 degrees, lay the molding flat on the table and cut to length. Keep the molding upside down.

The result.

Apply glue to the return...

and nail it in place. Ideally use three nails, two at the top and one at the bottom. This return will act as a stop and be most helpful when fitting and installing the rest of the crown.

With the miter saw angled in the opposite direction of the first corner and the molding upside down and backwards, make the cut with a slow, steady motion.

Walk the molding down...

These spring loaded corner clamps will hold the crown in place so I can work at the other end.

and mark the edge of the leg at the other end.

Fit the opposite corner...

and make any necessary adjustments.

and the lower edge of the main crown molding. Spread it with your finger.

Release the clamp and apply glue to the ends...

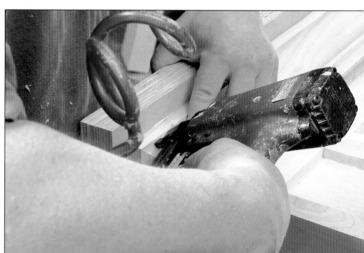

Put the crown in place and nail, moving from one end to the other. I first nail at the top, into the mantle top.

the upper edge...

Then I move to the bottom, into the leg.

As you move to the center be sure to angle the nail up to account for the recessed filler.

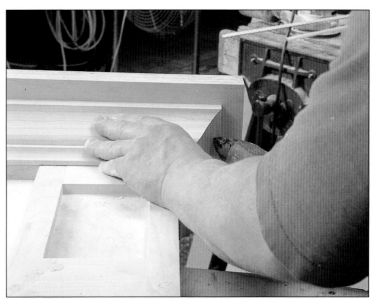

Glue and nail the return in place.

Alternate upper and lower nails as you work your way down the molding.

Clean up any glue seepage.

Mark the other return to length and cut it off.

One trick. If the mitered joint has a small gap in it, work some glue into the joint...

then burnish the joint with the round shaft of a screwdriver.

Rip and plane 3/4" x 1-1/2 nominal maple stock to 1/2" x 1 1/2". This will be used for the face molding of the mantel shelf. I finish this by giving it a cove, using a 5/8" radius core box bit. I set the router table to leave about 3/16" of fillet on the bottom edge of the molding. I use about three passes to get to the final shape. This helps prevent tear out and burning. Note the use of hold-down devices to keep my fingers away from the bit.

This closes up the gap nicely.

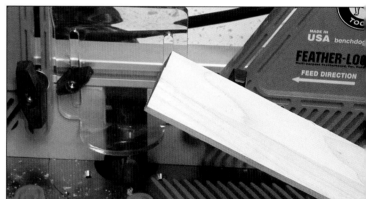

The result.

After knocking off the wood filler with 120 grit paper, go over the carcass with 150 grit. My goal is not to sand the wood but to even it out at the joints. I use light pressure, applying slightly more to the solid wood than to the veneer of the plywood.

The bullnose molding that goes across the bottom of the breastplate and around the legs is also routed from 1/2" stock that you will need to plane. I use a 1/4", quarter-round bit. This, used in two directions, will give you a better cut than a bullnose bit, with less chance of tear out. Set the router so that the bottom of the router bit barely touches the wood. We'll make one light cut, then move the fence back to make a deeper cut. Use at least two cuts to make this shape. Route one edge...

then turn it over and complete the bullnose. Adjust the fence and make the cut deeper

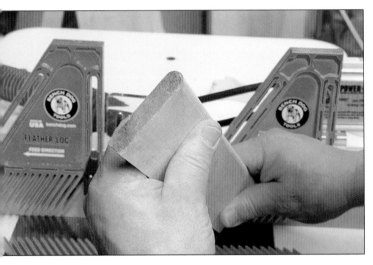

The result. It is best to do sanding now, before it is ripped, because you have something to hold onto.

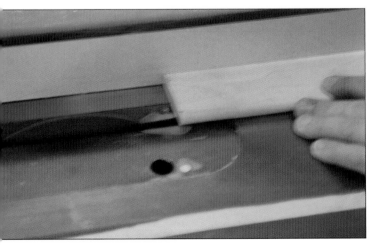

Rip the edge of the board to produce the bullnose molding. Keep the molded edge away from the fence, and set the blade 1/4" above the board, and the fence to leave a 3/8" molding.

The result.

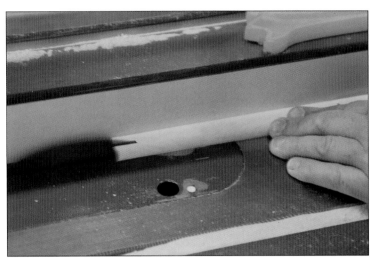

The trim molding for the face panels is cut from maple base shoe molding, 1/2" x 3/4". Because moldings are not readily available in every wood species, sometimes it is necessary to improvise like this. I rip away the square edge leave 7/16" on the curved edge. The depth of the molding at this point is 3/8", which will leave me a nice reveal at the edge of the panel. The molding for the top of the foot is the same maple base shoe, ripped to 1/2". This will leave it 1/2" x 1/2" and give a 1/4" step at the top of the foot.

Begin by applying the face molding to the mantel shelf by putting a 45 degree angle on a short piece of molding and on the joining end of the piece that goes across the front. Bring them together and mark the end pieces to length.

Trim the end piece, glue and nail it in place.

Cut, fit, glue, and nail the other end of the face molding.

Mark the face molding for the front and cut it a little long for fitting. Adjust to the correct length and cut at a 45 degree angle.

Progress.

Glue and nail the face molding to the front of the mantel shelf.

Before fitting the molding for the panels, I like to give it a good sanding. It is much easier now than after the moldings are installed. Working one panel at a time, cut the moldings. I prefer to cut the long pieces first, but it is not necessary. Dry fit all the pieces before gluing.

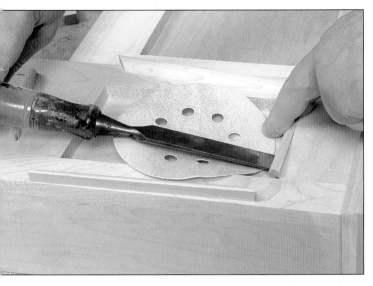

When you remove the piece, protect the surrounding wood.

When putting the molding in place be very careful not to get glue on surrounding surfaces.

This is a place where you want to be very careful of glue runovers. Run a bead of glue along the corner of the molding.

Install one corner.

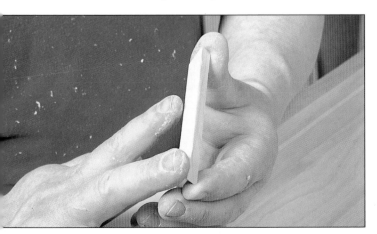

Spread the glue with your finger, removing the excess.

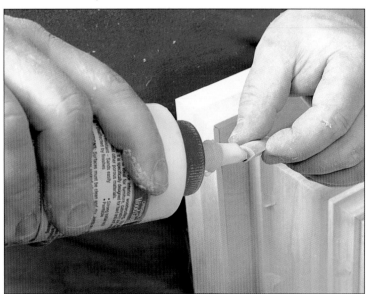

On the remaining two pieces, put a touch of glue on the end...

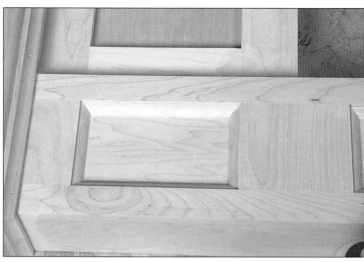

and a light spread of glue on the side that will be against the face. The sides do not need glue.

This creates a tight joint that needs few, if any, nails.

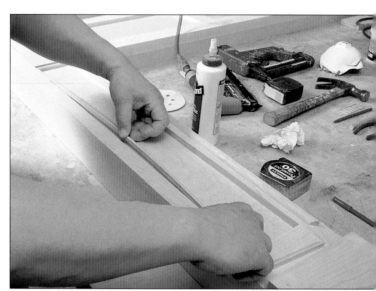

Apply the last two pieces together, pushing them into the corner.

Longer pieces with snug fits go in easily by bowing them slightly. They will "spring" into place.

Work them into place.

I change nail guns here. I am using a micro pinner, leaving less of a nail hole.

The micro pins are the same length as before, but are thinner than carcass nails. These are 23 gauge.

Mark the other end.

Repeat the process with each of the panels in the legs and breastplate.

Cut to length. Note that I am using a plywood backboard on the miter table. This reduces the chance of breakage.

Moving to the trim along the lower edge of the breastplate, cut one end to 45 degrees and hold in place.

Glue and nail so it is flush with the lower edge of the breastplate. Normally I start at one end and nail across, but in this case there is an odd hook in the half round, so I'm starting in the middle and working out.

Cut a 45-degree angle on the return and hold it in place to mark it. Chop it off with another 45-degree angle and adjust the fit.

and the cross-leg piece...

Cut a fresh 45-degree angle on the end of the piece that crosses the leg. With the return in place mark the length and cut.

and nail in place. This is a very visible piece, so take your time and get it right.

Glue in the return...

Hold the side return in place, mark it, and cut it.

Glue the return...

The molding at the top of the foot is the same as that used in the panels. Hold it in place, mark it, then cut it.

and nail in place. Repeat on the other side.

Glue and nail in place.

# Finishing

The results before finishing.

We took the mantel to a professional finishing shop. It has been secured to a movable dolly and placed in a ventilated spray booth.

Finishing can be done in a number of ways by hand or spray. In Portland, we are fortunately to have a shop that specializes in spray finishes. Here is Dan Standley as he begins the application of a clear lacquer finish. It is important to start with a clean, dust free surface.

Bend you knees, not your back, to achieve the best results when working on the lower parts.

Begin spraying "off the edge of the piece." This insures that your spray pattern will cover the edge.

Note that the installer keeps his spray gun at a consistent distance from the work. Don't forget to spray "off the edge" at the bottom.

The secret here is not to apply too much finish. It is important to keep your spray source the same distance from the work.

Make sure your spray hose is long enough and flexible. Note the distance from the work and the spray pattern. Too close and you will get runs, too far away and you create streaks. Practicing on a sample piece will help you get the best results.

Here's your sprayed mantle drying. The lacquer finish will give a "lifetime" finish. Easy to clean, it can be touched up if damaged.

Thanks to Keren and Dan from Spray Kote Finishing, Inc.

We made another mantel to hand finish. Supplies shown include sandpaper, in sheets, pads and discs, wood filler, nail set, tack cloth, gloves, wood finish and brushes.

This picture is of dried wood filler under our first top coat. Not good! This is what can happen to your work if you apply to much of the color-matched filler, don't find it and then apply a coat of finish over it. The fix is a time-consuming re-sanding and refinish. Hey, if it can happen to us it can happen to you!

Start by filling cracks with color matched wood filler. You may have to mix a couple of colors of filler to match the color of the wood. We use blue tape to prevent spread of filler. Wipe off excess filler while it is still wet.

Begin the sanding process with a random orbit rotary sander and 220 grit paper. We only work the flat surfaces. You might be tempted to "tip" your sander so as to sand the recessed areas. Don't do it.

Fill nail holes. If the nail is close to the surface, use the nail set and hammer to recess it a bit and fill. Be careful to avoid spreading the filler.

Here are the sanding accessories that will get into the moldings and hard-to-get-to places. Note the various shapes of devices that can hold a folded piece of sandpaper. Dowels can be useful; they are round and available in many diameters to fit molded profiles. You can cut or reshape any of these sandpaper holders to suit your needs.

Use a block to hold your paper. There are many types of blocks, including this scrap piece from the mantel

All right, you've sanded to 220 grit and you're done. Not quite. I like to give one last, light, sand, with the grain. You might call it superstition or overkill, but I think of this as cheap insurance.

Here we use a dowel to sand the inside of our coved crown molding. You can see how other shapes can be used to sand inside or outside of any curved surface.

Vacuum the dust. I usually vacuum first. A word of caution for those who might use an air compressor to blow off the dust. Some compressors blow trace amounts of oil and water in the air. This mix can stain your project, requiring another annoying, time consuming, resand.

Sanding where two grains come together. Sand with the grain. Where two grains come together, as in this photo, modify your block so you don't sand across grain. This minimizes scratches that might "telegraph" through your final finish.

Follow the vacuum with a tack cloth. Dust particles can create "bumps" in the finish. The tack cloth acts like a sticky clothes roller to remove dust particles.

I am not going to stain this mantle. However, if you wanted to stain yours, then use a test piece, like the one shown, to confirm that the color matches your décor. I apply a gelled stain with a clean cotton cloth. Wipe off excess.

Here's the completed test piece, still slightly wet. Give it overnight to dry to the true color. If you do stain your mantel you will wait 24 hours before a light sanding to 220 grit. Tack cloth again to remove dust and move on to the next step, the top coat, using the following instructions. Note that you can use a poly brush, brush or the clean rag for application of stain.

I'm using a semigloss urethane for a natural look. Apply with a poly brush or regular bristle brush according to your preference or availability. Light coats flow better so use small amounts and come back for more as needed. I usually dip a quarter inch of the brush into the finish for each application.

Working out from the center.

Finishing the molded trim.

Using a poly brush on the tilted areas can help prevent runs. Hint: don't "load" your brush. Light coats are best. You should be completely coated by now. This completes the first coat, except for a last "cheap insurance" coat.

While completely covered and still wet, I like to go over the finish very lightly just one last time. Note that you should plan enough time to cover the entire mantel without interruption. I squeegee most finish out of my brush and lightly drag the brush in the direction of the grain. I aim to start "off the edge" and don't lift my brush until I'm off the opposite side. I feel that this helps avoid lap marks. Think of this as a caress rather than a paint stroke. Go over the entire mantel. Take care to lift your brush where two grains come together. After this step you will wait 24 hours.

Follow the light sand with your tack cloth. Let's get rid of that dust.

Wait 24 hours for the finish to dry. You can get creative for this step.

You are ready for your second coat of finish. You will not use as much finish because this coat covers your previous coat. It doesn't have to penetrate the wood. Go lightly here. Put a small amount on your brush and "pull" it gently across the mantels surface. Remember to pull the brush with the grain. As one side of the brush runs out of finish I flip to the other side. When the brush is empty I dip a small amount and repeat until the mantel is covered. Again, while still wet, I make a last caressing pass. Let dry overnight.

Your first coat is dry. We will sand again, but this time we change grit to 320 (finer) and vary the pressure we use. You will now be sanding the thin coat of finish instead of the wood. Feel the surface prior to sanding. It will feel smooth but there will be some small "bumps". This is normal. As the wood dries tiny splinters that have been pressed into the wood by sanding can shrink and stick up. Dust from the air can settle on the finish creating tiny bumps. A light sanding, like the caress used for your final finish will remove those bumps. Sand with the grain. Watch the cross grain. Remember, it's just a caress.

We're done! Now it's just a matter of time (24 hours) until the mantle is dry.

Often the top and feet benefit from additional coats due to the wear they receive. Follow instructions for the second coat. Remember, thin coats, very light sanding, tack the dust and wait overnight between. Want a buffed finish? Wait one week to insure a hard finish and use buffers polish or wax.

Thanks, Steve Penberthy and Larry Welsh.

# Decorative Accents

In my previous book, *Step-by-Step to a Classic Fireplace Mantel*, I built the Multnomah Mantel. Over the years this has been a very popular model.

Although comments have been positive about the "build," people who have built the Multnomah have asked for suggestions on how to "dress it up."

The following are pictures of a carcass, like the one done for this mantel, decorated with fluted legs and a combination of readily available decorative wood accents. These accents completely change a mantel to fit your personal style or decore.

Here we applied a piece of fluted molding to the front of our carcass. Notice that our "foot" is flat stock applied over the fluted. Finish off the foot with a panel molding.

You can change the crown molding, modify the leg from flat to fluted, and create a division across the mantle by use of molding.

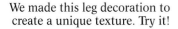

We made this leg decoration to create a unique texture. Try it!

The finished foot.

Where the fluted molding meets the center line of the mantel.

Another finished foot. Same carcass, different molding.

The cap and crown moldings have been changed and decorative accents added.

Create a different look to your cap piece by applying yet another molding profile.

Another view at the variety of "looks" that can be created by application of moldings.

Crown and cap treatment.

Shell and floral accent with plain crown molding.

Square accents lend a unique feel.

This is a smiliar carcass to the one used for this book. Here we have added fluted legs and a slightly different crown molding. The use of decorative accents above each leg and in the center will impart a different texture to your mantel. Note that we are showing two leg accents. You will use the same for both sides.

Here's a round accent and a larger molding used to give a more formal feel.

The fleur-de-lis accent used in the center is always nice.

You can combine accents for a pleasing combination.

The rope molding is applied above the fluted leg and across the front of the carcass.

Same carcass, here we use a dentil mold on the crown and a rope as a decorative center divider.

This crown includes a rope molding. We used a dentil molding and cove to create a different look.

Another combination of accent pieces.

Diamonds aren't just for special occasions.

Wow! This shell and floral centerpiece is majestic.

# Gallery

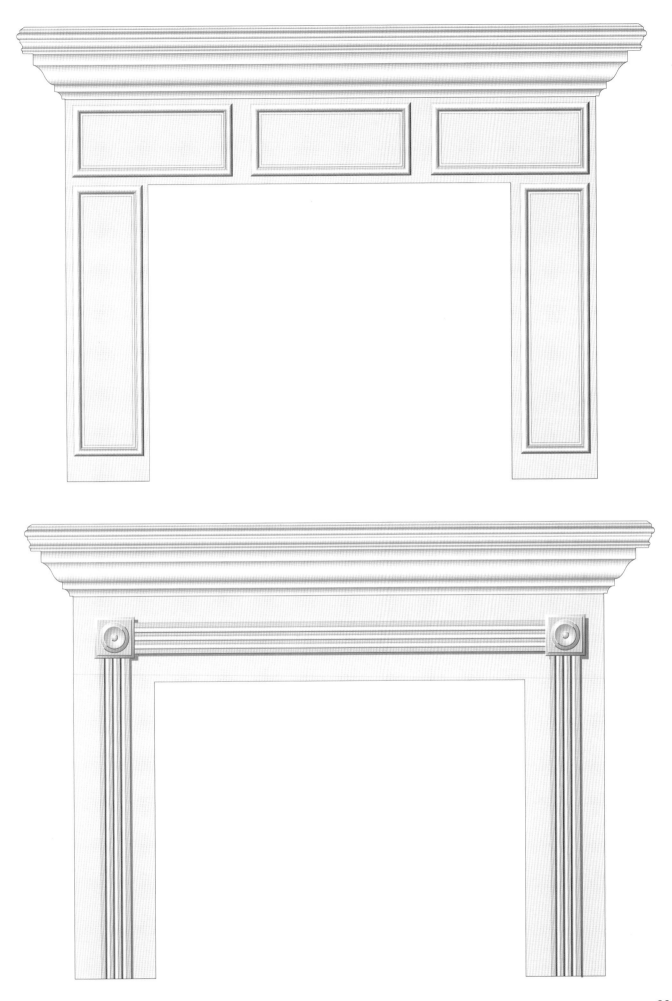

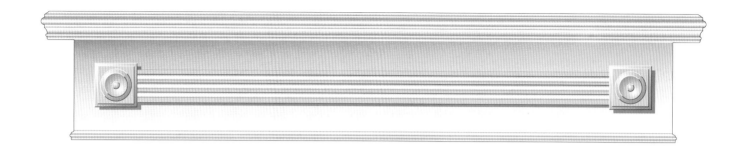

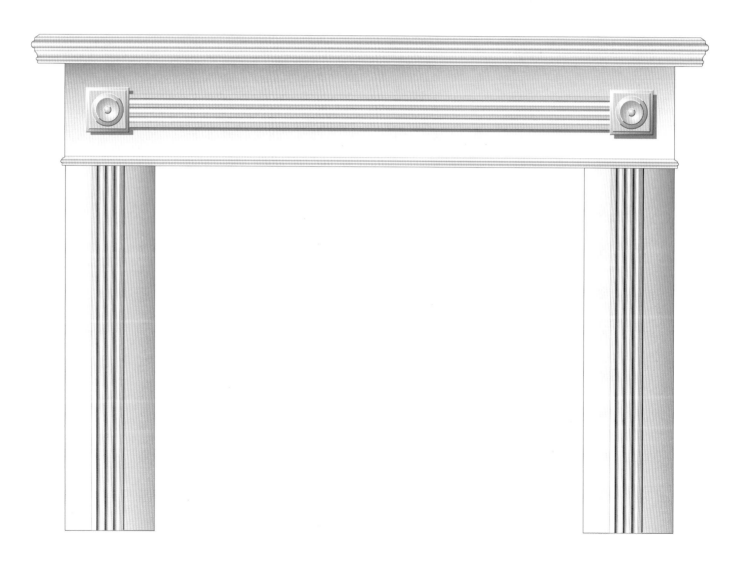

# Gallery of Finished Mantels

Courtesy of Jeff Metke, Metke Woodworking Inc., Lake Oswego, Oregon

Courtesy of Jeff Metke, Metke Woodworking Inc., Lake Oswego, Oregon

Courtesy of Jeff Metke, Metke Woodworking Inc., Lake Oswego, Oregon

Courtesy of Jeff Metke, Metke Woodworking Inc., Lake Oswego, Oregon

Courtesy of Jeff Metke, Metke Woodworking Inc., Lake Oswego, Oregon

Courtesy of Jeff Metke, Metke Woodworking Inc., Lake Oswego, Oregon

Courtesy of Jeff Metke, Metke Woodworking Inc., Lake Oswego, Oregon

Courtesy of Jeff Metke, Metke Woodworking Inc., Lake Oswego, Oregon

# Sources of Supply

## Molding

**Ferche Millwork**
Box 39
Rice, MN 56367
320-393-5700.
> Distributors of hardwood moldings nationwide. Dealer locator on website.
> • www.ferche.com

**Moulding and Millwork, Inc.**
> Distributors of mouldings nationwide and Canada. Dealer locator on website.
> • www.mouldingandmillwork.com.

**Woodcrafters Lumber Sales, Inc.**
212 NE 6th Ave.
Portland, OR 97232
800-777-3709
> Distributes moldings thru the Pacific Northwest. Distributors for Ferche and Moulding and Millwork. Fax 503-232-0511
> • www.woodcrafters.us@comcast.net

## Hardwood Lumber & Plywood

**Woodcrafters Lumber Sales, Inc.**
212 NE 6th Ave
Portland, OR 97232
800-777-3709.
> Distributes hardwood and plywood thru the Pacific Northwest. Fax 503-232-0511
> • www.woodcrafters.us@comcast.net

## Wood Finishes

**General Finishes**
P.O. Box 510567
New Berlin, WI 53151
800-783-6050.
> Nationwide manufacturer/distributor of finishing products for the furniture and cabinet trades.
> • www.generalfinishes.com

**Mohawk Finishing Products**
P.O. Box 22000
Hickory, NC. 28603
800-545-0047.
> Nationwide manufacturer/distributor of finishing products for the furniture and cabinet trade.
> • www.mohawk-finishing.com

**Woodcrafters Lumber Sales, Inc.**
212 NE 6th Ave
Portland, OR 97232
800-777-3709
> Distributes General Finishes and Mohawk Finishing Products thru the Pacific Northwest. Fax 503-232-0511
> • www.woodcrafters.us@comcast.net

## Sandpaper & Accessories

**Woodcrafters Lumber Sales, Inc.**
212 NE 6th Ave,
Portland, OR 97232
800-777-3709
> Complete woodworking accessory store. Hardwood lumber, plywood, molding, and veneers. Stock moldings including; alder, cherry, fir, hemlock, mahogany, maple, red and white oak, pine, poplar, walnut, finger joint, urethane foam and ultra light mdf. Millwork including custom molding to order, stair parts, corbels, carved architectural elements, flexible molding, mantels and columns. Router bits saw blades, shaper cutters, clamps, butcher blocks, drill bits and accessories. Sandpaper, abrasive cord, complete carving and turning selection. Sharpening supplies are a specialty. Delta, Jet, Powermatic, Shop Fox dealer. Thousands of titles of woodworking books and videos including all of Schiffer Publishing's woodworking related titles. A woodworker's paradise! Fax 503-232-0511.
> • www.woodcrafters.us@comcast.net

**Woodcraft Supply**
1177 Rosemar Rd.
Parkersburg, WV 26102
800-225-1153.
> Nationwide dealer of woodworking accessories. Hardwood lumber and veneers .Router bits, saw blades, clamps, drill bits and accessories. Lacquers, stains and finishing supplies. Sandpaper, abrasive cord, carving and turning tools available. Sharpening supplies are a specialty. Large selection of stationary and hand power tools. Many titles of woodworking books. Classes available.
> •www.woodcraft.com

**Rockler Woodworking and Hardware**
4635 Willow Drive
Medina, MN 55340
800-279-4441.
> Nationwide dealer of woodworking accessories. Cabinet and furniture hardware is a specialty. Hardwood lumber and veneers. Router bits, saw blades, clamps, drill bits and accessories. Lacquers, stains and finishing supplies. Sandpaper, abrasive cord, carving and turning tools available. Sharpening supplies are a specialty. Large selection of stationary and hand power tools. Many titles of woodworking books. Classes available.
> • www.rockler.com